Pigs on the Farm

by Mari C. Schuh

Consulting Editor: Gail Saunders-Smith, Ph.D.

Consultant: Jeff Ward
Director of Producer Education
National Pork Producers Council

Pebble Books

an imprint of Capstone Press
Mankato, Minnesota

Pebble Books are published by Capstone Press
151 Good Counsel Drive, P.O. Box 669, Mankato, Minnesota 56002
http://www.capstone-press.com

1 2 3 4 5 6 07 06 05 04 03 02

Library of Congress Cataloging-in-Publication Data
Schuh, Mari C., 1975–
    Pigs on the farm / By Mari C. Schuh.
    p. cm.—(On the farm)
    Includes bibliographical references (p. 23) and index.
    ISBN 0-7368-0993-7
    1. Swine—Juvenile literature. [1. Pigs.] I. Title. II. Series.
SF395.5 .S35 2002
636.4—dc21   2001001109

Summary: Simple text and photographs present pigs and how they are raised.

Note to Parents and Teachers

The series On the Farm supports national science standards related
to life science. This book describes and illustrates pigs on the farm.
The photographs support early readers in understanding the text.
The repetition of words and phrases helps early readers learn new
words. This book also introduces early readers to subject-specific
vocabulary words, which are defined in the Words to Know section.
Early readers may need assistance to read some words and to use
the Table of Contents, Words to Know, Read More, Internet Sites,
and Index/Word List sections of the book.

Table of Contents

tail

ears

snout

hooves

4

Pigs are farm animals.

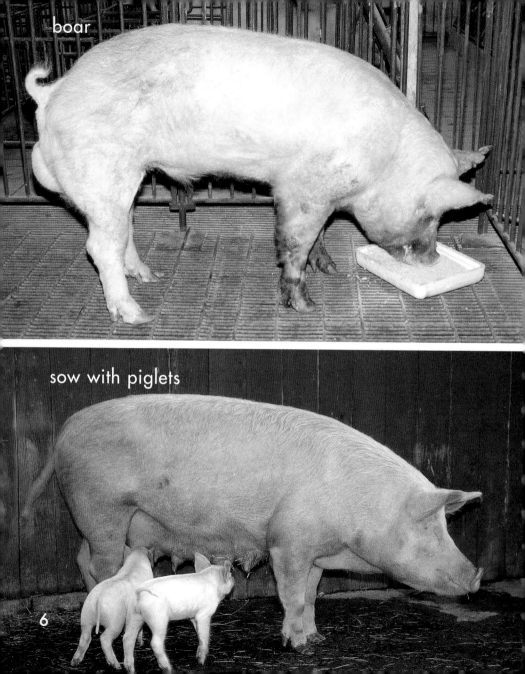

boar

sow with piglets

6

A male pig is called
a boar. A female pig is
called a sow. Young pigs
are called piglets.

Farmers raise pigs
for their meat.

Farmers feed pigs
corn and soybean meal.

Pigs live in pens. Farmers keep pens clean.

14

Some farmers spread pig manure on their fields. The manure helps crops grow.

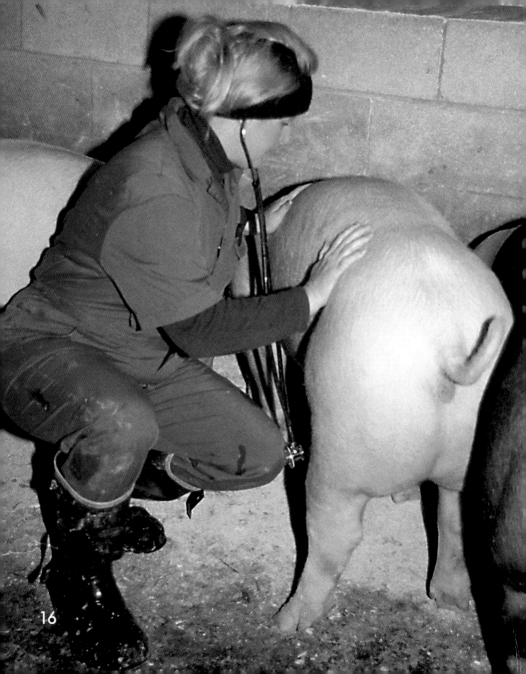

16

Veterinarians help
keep pigs healthy.

Some pigs roll in mud
to keep cool.

Pigs squeal.

Words to Know

crop—a plant grown for food

manure—animal waste; some farmers put pig manure on their fields as fertilizer.

meat—the flesh of an animal that can be eaten; people make the meat from pigs into ham, bacon, pepperoni, sausage, and salami.

raise—to care for animals as they grow and become older; farmers raise pigs for their meat; people also use parts of pigs to make leather, fertilizer, soap, chewing gum, and other products.

roll—to turn over and over; pigs cannot sweat, so they roll in mud to keep cool.

soybean—a seed that grows in pods on bushy plants; farmers feed pigs a corn and soybean meal mixture that has vitamins and minerals.

squeal—to make a shrill, high sound

veterinarian—a doctor who treats sick or injured animals

Read More

Bell, Rachael. *Pigs*. Farm Animals. Chicago: Heinemann Library, 2000.

Hansen, Ann Larkin. *Pigs*. Checkerboard Animal Library. Edina, Minn.: Abdo & Daughters, 1998.

Klingel, Cynthia Fitterer, and Robert B. Noyed. *Pigs: A Level Two Reader*. Wonder Books. Chanhassen, Minn.: Child's World, 2001.

Miller, Sara Swan. *Pigs*. A True Book. New York: Children's Press, 2000.

Internet Sites

North Carolina Pork for Kids
http://ncpork.org/educate.html

Pig Printout
http://www.EnchantedLearning.com/subjects/ mammals/farm/Pigprintout.shtml

Pork4Kids
http://www.pork4kids.com/kids/goHogWild.asp

Index/Word List

animals, 5
boar, 7
clean, 13
corn, 11
farm, 5
farmers, 9,
  11, 13, 15
feed, 11
female, 7
fields, 15

grow, 15
healthy, 17
keep, 13,
  17, 19
live, 13
male, 7
manure, 15
meat, 9
mud, 19
pens, 13

piglets, 7
raise, 9
roll, 19
sow, 7
soybean meal,
  11
squeal, 21
veterinarians,
  17
young, 7

Word Count: 72
Early-Intervention Level: 9

Credits

Heather Kindseth, cover designer; Heidi Meyer, production designer;
  Kimberly Danger and Deirdre Barton, photo researchers

David F. Clobes, Stock Photography, 10
Earthwatch Photography, 6 (top), 12, 16
Hans Reinhard/FPG International LLC, cover
Photri-Microstock, 6 (bottom); William Kulik, 4; D. Miliano, 20
Unicorn Stock Photos/B. W. Hoffmann, 8; Eric R. Berndt, 18
Visuals Unlimited/D. Cavagnaro, 1
Wildlands Conservancy/T. L. Gettings, 14

The author dedicates this book to her grandfather, the late Linus P. Brenner, who
raised hogs for more than 30 years in Mapleton, Iowa.